C000299659

BRITAIN IN OLD PHOTOGRAPHS

VENTNOR & DISTRICT

DONALD A. PARR

SUTTON PUBLISHING LIMITED

Sutton Publishing Limited
Phoenix Mill · Far Thrupp · Stroud
Gloucestershire · GL5 2BU

First published 1996

Copyright © Donald A. Parr, 1996

British Library Cataloguing in Publication Data
A catalogue record for this book is available from the
British Library.

ISBN 0-7509-1132-8

Typeset in 10/12 Perpetua.
Typesetting and origination by
Sutton Publishing Limited.
Printed in Great Britain by
Ebenezer Baylis, Worcester.

For many years Bonchurch has been regarded as a place of beauty. This photograph, taken in 1927, shows
the peace and tranquillity of the area.

CONTENTS

Introduction   5

1.   The People   7

2.   Around Ventnor   31

3.   Around the Villages: Chale, Godshill, Niton, Wroxall & Whitwell   51

4.   One Hundred Years of Transport   71

5.   Places of Worship   79

6.   Sports & Pastimes   95

7.   Blackgang & the Chine   107

     Acknowledgements   126

The Saunders family has lived in the Gatcombe/Niton area for several generations. As farm workers they have always been extremely popular, and George was known as 'Jolly'; he is seen here haymaking at Gatcombe Farm in 1917.

Boat trips, billiard halls and garden fêtes were the order of the day even in 1897, and then, just as now, locals would pause to 'put the world in order'. In those days, though, they could do so without being deafened by noise or choked by fumes from petrol engines.

INTRODUCTION

Ventnor, including St Lawrence, Bonchurch and the neighbouring villages, has been described as an 'extraordinary place with an unusual history'. Historians are still uncertain as to the derivation of the actual name 'Ventnor'. One suggestion is that the name originated from the Celtic 'gwent' and 'nor', meaning 'a white beach'; another is that the name may be of Danish origin. But wherever its roots lie, the town's attraction and situation remain superb in many ways.

Ventnor is shielded from the southerly gales of autumn and the north-west winds of spring, never too hot and never too cold. First-time visitors are astounded to see palm trees, myrtles, geraniums, heliotropes, verbena and petunias surviving the winter out of doors in the gardens of the houses and cottages. Because of a geological anomaly Ventnor is the one small area on the island in which this phenomenon occurs.

In the 1830s Ventnor was christened 'The English Madeira' by eminent physician Sir James Clarke, who highly recommended the climate to those who suffered from chest complaints. In the late 1800s the Royal National Hospital for Diseases of the Chest was built, which continued its successful function until it was demolished in 1964. Today the Botanical Gardens are situated on the 20 acre site, where some rare sub-tropical species, not found elsewhere in the British Isles, are grown.

Karl Marx spent the last years of his life in Ventnor, being treated by a local doctor for headaches and a bronchial condition. In 1878 a little boy came to stay in the town with his mother, and during a squall witnessed one of the worst disasters in the annals of the island's shipwrecks – the loss of over 300 men sailing back from Bermuda to Portsmouth on HMS *Eurydice*. The little boy was Winston Churchill, who recalls the scar this disaster left on his mind in his book, *My Early Life*.

Neighbouring Bonchurch became a haunt for the artists, authors and poets of the day. Swinburne and Keats took up residence, as did W.S. Gilbert and Charles Dickens, whose novel *Great Expectations* was started while he was staying there. Longfellow would drift in and out admiring the scenery, the residents and especially the chambermaid at the local hotel, and Tennyson, prior to moving to Freshwater on the western side of the island, stayed in Bonchurch long enough to be chased by a bevy of young women who once tore his wide-brimmed sombrero into shreds.

When travelling from West Wight to Ventnor today, it seems that little has changed. The leafy tunnel of the undercliff, a beautiful scenic approach, suddenly vanishes and St Boniface Down rears steeply to the left. Houses are built into several layers of the Down, terraced like an Alpine village. Drivers have to negotiate a series of twists and turns with alarming gradients, and strong stone retaining walls cling to the sides of the road. Down by the short esplanade and beach the Victorian-type houses with tiny gardens are also built into steep terraces, where one chimney is on a level with another front garden.

Ventnor is one of the most popular tourist resorts on the island today, the many holiday-makers attracted not only by the Mediterranean climate but also by the beauty of the area. As my other books in this series show, the Isle of Wight has seen many changes over the last century, from the advent of new shops and businesses in the towns to the arrival of the motor car. But the hospitality and warmth of the people and the charm and tranquillity that Ventnor retains have not changed, and it is these steadfast qualities that I hope this new book has captured.

THE PEOPLE

*A portrait of George 'Jolly' Saunders, taken in a
Newport studio, 1918. He died in 1938 at the age
of eighty-two.*

Alexander Green, known as 'Holy Joe', poses to have his photograph taken in Ventnor High Street in 1902. He lived the life of a troglodyte in a cave in Ventnor and survived by preaching, giving out tracts and accepting the food which was donated to him.

Mike Savatorie the organ grinder outside Newberry's store on the corner of Upper Gills Cliff Road and Newport Road, Ventnor, 1923. Newberry's store is now Crispy Fry.

The Ventucky Minstrels, a well-known Ryde concert group, 1952. The group invariably held their shows at Ventnor Town Hall, Albert Street.

To be a successful fisherman in 1870 you had to make all your own nets and pots. This picture, taken on the beach between Luccombe and Ventnor, demonstrates the art of making lobster pots.

Before mechanization farm workers faced many backbreaking tasks. This photograph shows Art Moses at Wroxall in 1930 carrying two heavy buckets with the aid of a yoke.

A threshing machine at Southford Farm, Whitwell, 1940. Left to right: Jacob Saunders (son of 'Jolly'), Will Hunt, Jim Dyer.

Jacob Saunders spent most of his working life at Southford Farm. It was always said that the Saunders men and the land were as one. This photograph was taken in 1942.

For many years four cottages in Southford Lane, Redhill, were forced to share one well. Every summer the residents hoped that the authorities would lay on mains water, but the argument was over cost and who would pay. Meanwhile residents, including Mrs Newington (née Saunders), daughter of Jacob, had to rely on buckets, which were lowered on a 20 ft length of rope.

During the Second World War Ventnor was to play its part as one of the main radar sites for the south of England. In addition, the men who did not join the armed services formed their own home guard unit. Included here, in 1944, are Mr Allan and Ernest Carley.

Ventnor fire crew on parade for the wedding of Charlie Coleman, 1924. Back row, left to right: Ben Jacobs, Charlie Coleman, Charlie Whiteman, Fred Nobbs (driver), Bob Spenser (First Officer). Front row: Horace Crump, Joe Jacobs, 'Mac' McLean, Michael Wheeler, Clem Grant (Third Officer) and Tom Pearson (Second Officer).

By 1928 many of the taverns were using the new conveyance, the charabanc, for their outings. The Volunteer at Ventnor hired this charabanc, 'Red Chief', owned by Nash coaches. The party includes Mrs Humphries, Arthur P. Hill, Harry Humphries, Mr Carter, Charlie Taylor, Doug Calman, Penny Humphries, 'Soldier' Harvey, Bert Kingswell, George Walton, Archie Coleman, Jim Smith (in peak cap), George Walton, Bert Brown, Mr Scott, Alec Bull, 'Musher' Sheath, Tom Coleman and Bob Dore.

Many other groups went on outings. This one was visiting Godshill in 1939 and is believed to have included Jennifer Smith and Bertram Pinner.

The Wheeler family, who fished at Chale Bay, 1918. Back row, left to right: Dot Wheeler, Ernest Wheeler, Alice Wheeler, 'Granny' Wheeler, Mrs Bridden and Ted Bridden (private detective to HM Queen Mary), Rene Cheek, Bert Kingswell. Middle row: Ethel Chiverton, Mrs Bridden, Mr Chiverton, Mrs Chiverton, Mrs Kingswell with Molly on her lap. Front row: two Bridden children, Fred Nobbs, Phyllis Nobbs.

Wroxall School. The group includes Mrs Bertha Ford (teacher), Mr Francis (headmaster), Polly Booker (back row, seventh from left), Emily Booker (second row, fifth from left), Lucy Orchard (to her right) and Bert Whittington (front right). (The date of the photograph is not known.)

Fred Kempton at Southford Farm, having prepared one of the great shire horses for a ploughing match, 1957.

Wroxall County Primary School orchestra, 1905. The third girl from the left is Annie Morris, on the far right is Lillian Whittington and the teacher is Mr Francis.

A garden party held at The Knoll, Ventnor, on 19 July 1933. Included in the group are Florence White, Mrs Grady, Ivy Chiverton, Mrs Brackett and Miss Hearn.

With the onset of the First World War, many villages throughout England saw their menfolk volunteer for the armed services. Chale was no exception. The children were given time off from school to join their parents to wish the volunteers *bon voyage* and a safe return. Believed to be in the photograph are Frank Reynolds, Olive Sprake, Jim Cheek (who owned the house in the background), John and Charlie Cheek and Will Sprake.

Godshill School children with trays of eggs. We have been unable to find out the significance of this, so if any reader has any information please let the school know.

The following four photographs show pupils at Godshill School. Unfortunately we are unable to name any of those pictured, but should you recognize any child or teacher the school would be delighted to know. The photographs above and below are of class 1 and class 2, *c.* 1914.

Above, a photograph dating from 1906; below, 1916.

A group from Niton Methodist Church, 1911. Among those shown are Mrs Morris (Sunday school superintendent), Mr and Mrs A. Salter, Elizabeth Saunders, Mr Aisher, Mrs Saunders, Walter Cotton and Henry Hawkins.

Another group from the church, 1904. Included here are Jane and William Jackson, Eliza and Walter Cotton, Francis and Harry Salter, Alfred Salter, Mrs Peach, Harry Simmonds and John Barnes.

The boys and girls of St Boniface were known for their polite behaviour, and the school for the high standard set. Unfortunately we were unable to find the names to fit the faces, but the photographs are believed to have been taken in 1902.

This is probably Wroxall Sunday school, 1910, but we have not been able to ascertain the location of the outing or any names.

An Easter Monday outing from Roud Chapel, 1921. Included in the photograph are Harry Brennon, Mrs Plumbley, Mrs Butcher, Mrs Lacey, Mr and Mrs Tutton, Miss Gird, Arthur Attril, Mrs McCumley from Wroxall and Olive Saunders, Jacob's daughter. The chapel opened in 1859.

Many of the long-term patients at the Royal National Hospital for Diseases of the Chest were encouraged to work out of doors as part of their treatment. To some, whose stay may have been anything up to twelve months, this must have seemed like a full-time occupation.

Patients in the great hall sitting down to Christmas dinner, 1947. Understandably, because of the confidentiality of patient records we were asked not to name anyone.

This picture illustrates the severity of school life at the turn of the century. Although writing, the children at the National School in Albert Street, Ventnor, have their backs straight and their heads held high.

The madness of the early days of aviation pioneering. In 1910 hundreds of people climbed to the top of St Boniface to help with the Bristol box kites.

This photograph is thought to have been taken at the same time as those on page 20, and again, should anyone have any details of the pupils or the teachers, please inform Godshill School.

Visitors and residents alike would flock to watch the harvesting of the mackerel, which would be brought ashore in their thousands.

In the early days of the coastguard, training comprised rocket drill and the setting up of sheerlegs and ropeways to practise the movement of men and equipment over long distances of cliff tops and rugged terrain. These four photographs, taken by Mr J. Dore in 1900 and using the old glass-plate camera, give a good insight into the vigorous training which these men undertook at Steephill.

With the snow of 1952 came disruption to the island transport system.

The staff of Blackgang Chine, 1920. On the left are Mrs Isolene Dabell and her three lady helpers; the elderly gent is Bert Coles, head gardener, and the tall man is his assistant. This was the entire staff of Blackgang Chine in those days.

SECTION TWO

AROUND VENTNOR

The Bijou Cinema in the High Street. This was Ventnor's first cinema.

Mr Milne, an early photographer, lining up his cameras to photograph the road to Ventnor, 9 August 1902.

The Marine Hotel in Ventnor, now demolished, enjoyed uninterrupted sea views. In its heyday this hotel was fully booked by those wishing to take full advantage of the 'beneficial' sea breezes.

Mac Fisheries in Ventnor High Street, 1930. On the left is manager Alf Farrant. Note the prices: 1s for a rabbit or 1 lb of turbot, or 3s 9d for game birds. Those were the days, my friends – or were they?

The Victorian ladies and their escorts would promenade along the pier. This photograph, taken by John Dore in about 1900, clearly shows that this sort of exercise took place whatever the weather.

Wheelers Bay, showing the fishermen's cottages, *c.* 1900. Those living here must have taken the full force of any gales blowing in from the sea.

The newly constructed pier, *c.* 1911. The bathing huts along the water's edge are still in evidence.

The pathway, known as Ventnor Cascade, which leads from the esplanade into town.

St Boniface Down makes a fine backdrop in this view of a Southern Vectis coach travelling along Ocean View Road towards Mitchell Avenue, *c.* 1930.

Those of us who regularly use Ventnor Cascade will find it hard to recognize this section of the seafront, photographed in about 1912.

Many things have changed during the last ninety years but not Trinity Road in Ventnor. Several features in this picture are still recognizable today.

This undated view, looking west over the town, makes one realize just how much property has been built to make the modern Ventnor we know today.

There is a remarkable resemblance between these two school buildings, although they were built many years apart. The top picture shows the National School in Albert Street, now demolished, and below is the County School in Lisson Road, taken in 1923. During the last war this school was thought to be too near the radar masts of St Boniface and therefore likely to be within a target area of enemy aircraft. The children were moved to a temporary school set up in Steephill Castle.

Even the sub-tropical climate of Ventnor occasionally suffers the rigours of winter. Looking west, this picture shows the esplanade during the heavy snow of December 1950.

The High Street on the same day. This certainly was not the sort of weather in which to be out shopping!

The snow made it hard for even the toughest dog to get about, *c.* 1956.

Steephill Castle amid the trees, before the Second World War. A hayrick is on the site of the present cricket ground.

This attractive building is the keeper's lodge in Ventnor Park, pictured during the heavy snow of 1909. At that time the park keeper was 'Walt' Butt.

Gill's, a well-known Ventnor butcher's in the High Street, 1920. Later the shop was taken over by Mr Smith. The gentleman in the doorway is believed to be Tom Mills, who worked there for many years.

Ventnor esplanade, presumably photographed from a boat, 1900. On the left is The Queens Hotel and next door is The Esplanade, which was recently destroyed by fire.

Ventnor esplanade, *c.* 1893. The small boating pond was destined to become the paddling pool containing a raised map of the island, beloved by thousands of children over the years.

Putting the finishing touches to the Jubilee Arch across Upper High Street, Ventnor, ready for the celebrations of Queen Victoria's Diamond Jubilee, 1897.

Ventnor beach and esplanade, *c.* 1870. Note the bathing machines and the modest mode of dress, even for the beach.

On the beach at Ventnor near la Falaise is this peculiar building known as 'Old Britannia's hut'. A well-known eccentric lady lived in it for many years until the late 1950s, when she was forced by the authorities to leave for reasons of safety and hygiene. The old lady, whose real name was Olivia Parkes, was popularly known as 'Old Britannia'.

The Old Manor House in The Grove, Ventnor, used in 1900 as a Victorian tea garden. This fine building was originally known as Ventnor Farm House and was built in about 1600. After the First World War it was closed as a tea garden and converted into two houses. Recently, however, it was converted into a single house again by its present owners, the Plumridge family, who are property and antique dealers.

Taken from the original glass plate by John Dore, this photograph, dated 1908, shows the splendour of Bonchurch pond. Little seems to have altered in the intervening ninety or so years.

A view of the esplanade, looking east, 1890.

This picture was also taken in 1890 but from the sea, and shows the ruggedness of the cliffs just east of the promenade.

The Royal National Hospital for Diseases of the Chest, opened in the mid-1860s by Doctor Arthur Hassall. The hospital buildings were linked by over a quarter of a mile of corridors. The establishment closed in 1964 and the site is now the Ventnor Botanical Gardens.

The Queen Mary hedge at St Lawrence became a tourist attraction for many holiday-makers. The topiarian placed a tin and wooden chute from the road to a collection box at the hedge so that money could be donated to the RNLI.

A very early view of Ventnor taken from a woodcut, believed to have been the work of Brannon, *c.* 1822.

The Pond, Bonchurch, Nr. Ventnor.

Bonchurch pond was the subject of this postcard, which was sent to Miss Hill of Gloucester in October 1913.

The Royal Hotel first opened its doors in 1832. As most of the customers arrived by boat the hotel would send down horses for the guests and the boat men would carry their baggage up to the hotel. Queen Victoria was a frequent visitor to the Royal.

This view of Ventnor seafront also appears on the front cover. Taken in about 1910, it shows the different changing huts for ladies and gentlemen.

Ploughing at Wacklands Farm, *c.* 1932. Before the modern tractor was used, ploughing was undertaken with shire horses such as these.

This undated picture was taken from the land to the west of Ventnor. It shows a desolate scene, which readily conjures up images of smuggling.

AROUND THE VILLAGES: CHALE, GODSHILL, NITON, WROXALL & WHITWELL

Children making their way down Church Hill, Godshill, 1919. Certainly today children could not walk safely hand in hand along the road in such a carefree manner.

The village store has been the hub of most communities and Chale Green is no exception. This picture was taken in 1951, when the store not only sold groceries but petrol, and alongside was a small butcher's.

Chale, 1913. On the left is Lower House Dairy, which was the first meeting-place of Chale Methodists in 1912.

Chale High Street, 1903. The scene is very different today.

This unique photograph was taken from the tower of Chale Church and shows the adjacent village shop and houses, 1901.

Sprakes Brewery, situated at the crossroads at Chale Green, in front of which was The Star. Sprakes was responsible for most of the ale drunk in the region, and even stronger stuff was pumped through a hole in the hearthstone from an illicit cask below.

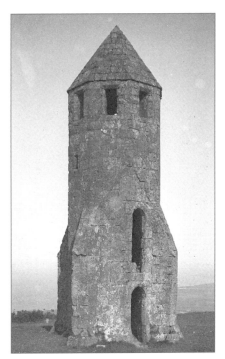

The Hoy Monument, a 72 ft obelisk erected to commemorate the visit in 1814 of Tsar Alexander I of Russia.

The Pepper Pot stands on what is commonly called 'Chale Mountain' (see below).

The Salt and Pepper Pots on Chale Mountain. In 1314 Walter de Godeton was lord of the manor at Chale. During that year a French ship carrying casks of good wine foundered and broke up on Atherfield Ledge. Locals seized the cargo and sold it to de Godeton but the wine belonged to the Monastery of Livers in Picardy. The Pope preferred a charge of sacrilege against de Godeton, who was made to build a lighthouse and lookout post.

St Catherine's Lighthouse was built in the nineteenth century to replace the two inadequate structures on St Catherine's Down which were frequently obscured by mists. The original lighthouse was built in 1840 as a direct result of the loss of the *Clarendon* at Blackgang on 11 October 1836.

Another view of the complete complex of St Catherine's Lighthouse, *c.* 1939. It is no longer manned and is instead fully automated.

The Buddle Inn at one time was an important wireless telegraphy station for shipping, but is now a successful and popular inn catering for locals and holiday-makers alike. Nearby Puckaster Cove and Reeth Bay have a rich history: the Romans shipped their cargos of Cornish tin from there, King Charles II landed at Puckaster Cove during a storm on 1 July 1675, and smuggling was rife until well into the nineteenth century.

Cripple Path, which runs from the Undercliffe to Niton, *c.* 1903. The climb is fairly difficult, which is why benches are provided half-way up. It is supposedly the path by which pilgrims found their way to the shrine of the Virgin Mary at Whitwell, and the name is said to derive from 'crooked' or 'crippled' path.

Niton High Street, 1907. It is interesting to see that Baverstock's general store was open even then.

Chale Bay mackerel have long been famous. After the catch was sorted the fish was taken round the villages and sold to the cry of 'Chale Bay Maackerel!'. The photograph dates from about 1910.

This landslide at Niton on 26 July 1928 was not unexpected, as warning notices had been erected as early as February of that year. It was estimated that between 100,000 and 200,000 tons of rock fell, with individual boulders weighing up to 80 tons.

The quiet High Street of Wroxall, *c.* 1910.

The Supply Stores, previously Wroxall Bakery, 1921. The stores were owned by Mr Bull and Mr Blake and were the mainstay of the village for many years. The gentleman standing in the doorway is Les Churt, a member of staff.

Wallis baker's shop and its horse-drawn delivery cart, Wroxall, 1922. The local constabulary may be looking for a possible parking charge. Opposite is the Queen Victoria jubilee monument.

The village of Wroxall as seen from Appuldurcombe House, which was destroyed by a land mine during the last war.

These two photographs show men working on the pipeline for the Chillerton Wroxall waterworks, probably between the wars.

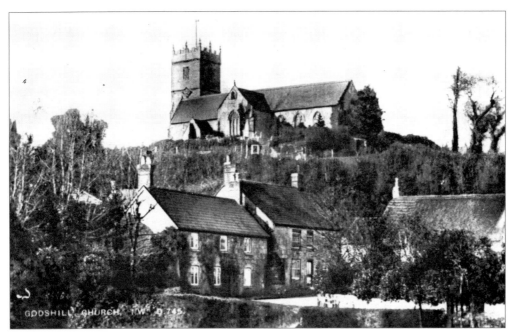

Above and below, the half-timbered cottages of Godshill huddled on a steep mound; behind is the large church with its fine perpendicular tower. The top picture dates from about 1912, and the lower one from about 1890.

Whitwell post office and grocery shop at the beginning of the century, when George Phillips was postmaster. The billboard on the wall advertises the Isle of Wight Central Railway. At that time Whitwell had its own station, connecting it with both Newport and Ventnor.

Godshill village and church, 1920. Legend has it that when the church was built, the foundations were laid at the bottom of the hill, not far from the last house to the left of the picture, but during the night the Godshill pixies moved both the materials and the foundations to the top of the hill.

John Abbott with his pony and trap, which served not only as a taxicab but also to transport general goods and parcels. They are pictured outside Godshill School, 1916.

The Fighting Cocks at Hale Common, before alterations in the 1960s.

Horringford station is on the periphery of the area covered by this book. It was closed by the Beeching axe in the 1960s.

Godshill village, *c.* 1930. This quiet country scene is a far cry from the Godshill of today.

THE SHOW COTTAGE

Patronized by H.M. Queen Mary and H.R.H. Princess Beatrice.

Genuine Antiques

Fine collection of early period furniture in re-constructed 16th-century building.

GODSHILL

ISLE OF WIGHT

A business card for the Godshill Show Cottage, featured opposite.

One of the earliest pictures found of Godshill, believed to have been taken in the 1870s.

The Show Cottage, 1940. This was owned by a Mrs Vapini and was truly something to see. For years she charged 6d to have a look round and people would come for miles, including Queen Mary and Princess Beatrice. Glass tubes were suspended from the ceiling into which visitors would be asked to put their sixpences. The cottage itself dates back to the 1500s.

The Russell brothers road gravelling at Yard Farm, Wroxall, 1920.

Appuldurcombe House, once owned by the celebrated Worsley family, was ruined by a land mine which exploded nearby during the Second World War. The mansion once contained a profusion of treasures acquired from the Orient. The Benedictines of Solesmes exiled themselves here from 1901 until they purchased Quarr Abbey House.

ONE HUNDRED YEARS
OF TRANSPORT

The first articulated lorry on the island, seen here in 1922. It was a solid-tyre chain-driven Scammel.

The last train at Ventnor West, 13 September 1952. The morning crew take on water.

Crinnage Coaches of Ventnor would often have all its vehicles at Alum Bay. Here the drivers are posing for a works photograph, c. 1930.

This rare photograph shows an Avro aeroplane. The pilot somehow lost his bearings and, running low on fuel, landed at Ventnor on 17 October 1919. Boatmen were persuaded to fetch some fuel from the nearest garage and the plane took off again, no harm done. One of the lads in the picture is Fred Nobbs, who related the story.

Sharpe's outing in a Dennis coach, Ventnor, 9 July 1919. As coaches of the day had solid tyres and the roads were rutted, each ride was one to remember. Among those pictured are Bill Pitts (driver), Mr A.J. Sharpe, Mr Redder, Mr Westmore, Harold Lauder and Frank Grant.

Ventnor seafront at low tide, c. 1915. It was the practise for small sailing craft to be beached, when their sails would be hoisted to dry.

The Booth family, who owned the manor-house, also ran a Ventnor bakery. Pictured here by their model 'T' Ford delivery van in 1915 are Miss Drake and Miss Fosh, who drove and delivered.

The first motor charabanc on the island, belonging to Crinnage, 1913. It was a Minerva, built by Martin Bros of Ventnor. The driver is Charlie Drake.

In 1929 Crinnage obtained a rigid Scammel with a gas-burning engine. Anthracite was used to produce the gas, although not in large enough quantities to enable the lorry to negotiate some of the island's hills, especially in the Ventnor area. At these times it had to revert to petrol. It also had to tow the gas-burning plant wherever it went.

Ventnor railway station soon after it opened in 1866. It fell to the Beeching axe in 1966, just one hundred years later.

Many of the hotels in Ventnor became staging posts for the stagecoaches in the late 1800s. The coaches were mostly open to the elements. It is interesting to note that the coachmen wore top hats and frock coats, and that ladders were available for passengers to embark and alight.

Pub outings were common in the early part of this century. This photograph is believed to show one of Jack Wavell's Golden Road charabancs, 1921.

PLACES OF WORSHIP

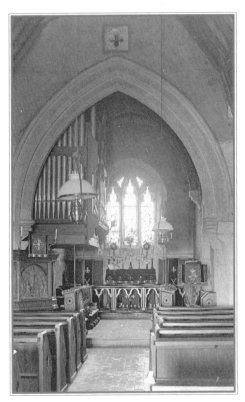

The interior of Chale Church before the organ was moved. The organ started life on the left, as here, but in 1932 the whole console and pipes were transferred to the right of the altar.

This early nineteenth-century engraving is of the parish church at Chale with its Norman tower. Built by Hugo de Vernon, lord of the manor of Chale, it has a list of rectors dating from 1269. In 1939 Count Adam Karolyi, the only son of the first president of the Hungarian Republic, who was exiled here during the Horthy regime, died in an aircraft accident. The ex-president died in France in 1955 in his eighty-first year but was brought to Chale to be laid to rest beside his son. Their remains were exhumed in 1961 and re-interred in a stately mausoleum in Budapest, near the body of Kossuth, the famous Hungarian patriot. The then rector of Chale, Revd C. Sinclair, was invited to the state funeral and remained in Budapest for a week as a guest of the Hungarian foreign minister.

Roud Baptist Chapel, 1921.

Re-opened in 1918 after the First World War, here the chapel is decorated for the harvest festival. Unfortunately, in common with many country places of worship, it was forced to close in 1971 after giving 112 years' service to the Baptist Church and the local community.

Godshill Church was struck by lightning on 14 January 1904. For months afterwards, local people were analysing the occurrence and many country folk were blaming it on divine retribution. However, the rural dean was quoted as saying: 'That's ridiculous. Why should God want to destroy His own house?'

There are a number of monuments to the Worsley family in Godshill Church. Here are just two of them, to Sir Robert Worsley, 4th Baronet, and to his brother Henry. Both monuments were erected in 1741.

One of the local characters was Capt. Worsley, who spent his time around the village after retiring in 1929. Here he is in July 1930 performing a task which he had rather assumed than been appointed to do, that of showing visitors around the church and getting a donation of 6d from each person. Needless to say he would specifically point out all the family monuments in the church.

The interior of St Luke's Chapel at the Royal National Hospital, Ventnor. Some of the stained-glass windows were removed before the demolition of the chapel in the 1960s. They were resited in St Lawrence Old Church and rededicated in the presence of HM Queen Elizabeth The Queen Mother.

Sandford United Methodist Church, *c.* 1928.

Laying the foundation stones of the church, 1910.

Niton Methodist Church was built in 1863. Local builders were invited to tender to undertake the work and the winning tender was that of Messrs Moses and Walden of Ventnor. The quotation for building a church with a seating capacity of one hundred was £181 10s 0d, which was accepted on 26 October 1863.

Chale Church, 1950. A church has stood on the same site since before Norman times. Gifford, Bishop of Winchester, is known to have dedicated a church on 1 December 1114, but hardly a trace of it remains. Only on the north wall of the present church are there signs of a door and window.

The Roman Catholic church of St Wilfred's in Ventnor has stood on the same site for many years. Pictured here is the high altar.

This picture, taken from a glass plate, shows St Wilfred's before the building of the school house, 1890.

Interior views of St Wilfred's. As in most towns throughout England, there is one Roman Catholic church serving one community. St Wilfred's offers a friendly welcome to all, residents and holiday-makers alike.

The Military, or Coastal, Road leading towards Chale Church, 1900. Geologically the island has layers of blue slipper, a clay on top of greensand, which crumbles after heavy rain. It is reckoned that on average at least 1 ft of land annually is lost to the encroaching sea, but in some years devastating landslips can alter the coastline overnight.

The interior of Chale Church, c. 1932. The late Mr Arnold Hearn, a New York businessman, donated many of the present windows and rebuilt the organ. He was a descendant of Revd John Hearn, one-time incumbent of the church.

The congregation of Chale Methodist Church, 10 June 1936. Unfortunately we have been unsuccessful in finding out any names but we understand that it was on the occasion of a rather significant anniversary.

Also photographed at this gathering was a group of Methodist ministers and their wives. Believed to be among them were Revd and Mrs C. Bennett and Revd and Mrs R. Turner.

The parish church of St Andrew, Chale, 1908. One of its bells is inscribed 'Sancea Margareta' and is dated 1314, but the dedication suggests that it was secondhand when installed in the fifteenth century. It was cast some two hundred years earlier by Peter de Weston's partner, who simply signed himself 'R'.

A rare picture of the road leading from Shanklin to Godshill via Sandford, c. 1897. For many who attended regular worship at that time All Saints', Godshill, was the nearest church, and for those who were unable to afford a carriage, the trek there on a wet day would prove rather a labour of love.

The old church of St Boniface at Bonchurch, 1893. It is a simple church with simple tablets and stones, and was restored by Percy Stanley in 1922. This photograph, taken from a glass plate, shows the church before the start of restoration. Most of the architecture is still Norman.

The old church of St Boniface at Bonchurch, *c.* 1922. Tradition has it that the monks of Lyre landed at Monks Bay in the eighth century and founded the first church of St Boniface at Bonchurch (or, as it was then known, Bonecerce). A coin of Aethelwulf, father of Alfred the Great, was unearthed there.

A better view of the churchyard, *c.* 1922. Among the trees and within sight of the sea (which is now much nearer because of erosion) are the headstones of farmers, quarrymen and fishermen. Prestigious visitors include Charles I, who attended the funeral of Sir Ralph Chamberlayne. Algernon Charles Swinburne was christened here, and Dickens and Keats, sometimes joined by Tennyson, worshipped at the church.

KINDLY HANG IN LOBBY.

High Street Methodist Church,
WROXALL, I.W.

PRELIMINARY NOTICE.

Welcome to the Opening Services and Dedication of the New School Hall and Vestry, on Whit-Monday, June 5th, commencing at 2-30 p.m.

PREACHER and SPEAKERS:

Rev. Wm. JACKSON, M.A., Ex-President of Conference.

Rev. A. J. CONIBEAR, Chairman, Portsmouth District.

Mr. W. H. STONEMAN and Others.

Public Tea.   Music by S.A. Band.

Great Thanksgiving Service 7 p.m.

£250 needed to open free of debt

Gifts gratefully received.

Rev. Hy. PARSONS,
MADEIRA ROAD,
VENTNOR, I.W.

A poster for High Street Methodist Church, Wroxall, announcing a service of dedication for the new school hall and vestry on Whit Monday, 5 June 1933. We are pleased to say that the target of £250 was achieved and the hall opened free of debt.

Wroxall Methodist Church was opened in February 1887 with seating for two hundred people. The first chapel was a wooden structure erected by the Bible Christians in about 1823. It was followed by a more substantial building in 1868 on a site opposite the corner of High Street and Manor Road. Known as The Bible Christians' Chapel, it was used as the Methodist Sunday school rooms until it closed in 1933.

This picture, taken in 1929, shows the 1868 chapel tucked away behind the tennis courts. During the Second World War it was badly damaged by blast from a stray enemy bomb and had to be demolished. The land was purchased by Mr Gough, who built a house and a shop selling fruit and vegetables. Soon part of it became a butcher's. Both shops are still running under the name of Heal's.

SPORTS & PASTIMES

The official opening of Ventnor Bowling Club green on 20 May 1914.

A meeting of the foxhounds in Chale Green, 1907. Please note that the policeman on his bicycle was not part of the hunt!

Ventnor Annual Gymkhana, 8 September 1909. Even in the early 1900s a local gymkhana was regarded as a great day out, with events for all the family. Here a bicycle race is in progress.

The Godshill tug-of-war team won the Isle of Wight heavyweight championship in 1947. Included here are Reg Andrews, Percy Scott, Phil Thatcher and Art Cheverton.

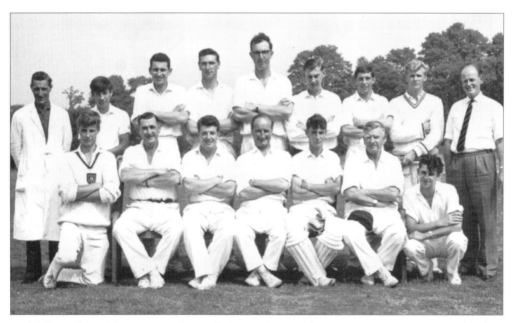

Godshill Cricket Club, 1964. Back row, left to right: G. Thorne, T. Jones, K. Day, C. Thatcher, B. Thatcher, R. Mew, L. Barlow, V. Radcliffe, P. Domoney (scorer). Front row: D. Charles, R. Blow, G.R. Thorne, D.J. Childs (captain), C. Hayles, A. Mackett, R. Denness.

Godshill Cricket Club, 1951. Back row, left to right: Mr Bailey, A.E. Coddington, N. Rosten, W.J. Bell, P. Clarkson, B. Thatcher, G. Rann, R. Hood-Bailey, E. Mitchell. Front row: E. Sloper, C.J. Hayles, G. Thorne, J. Robinson (president), R.A. Blow (captain), D. Charles.

Godshill Cricket Club, 1962. Back row, left to right: R.W. Mew, D. Charles, N. Thorne, B. Thatcher, K. Day, G.R. Thorne, C. Hayles, A. Domoney. Front row: G.H. Thorne, R. Blow, D.J. Charles (captain), C. Thatcher, A. Mackett.

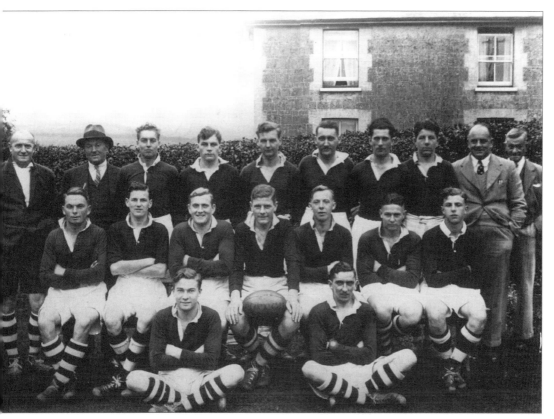

Ventnor Rugby Football Club, 1937/8 season. Back row, left to right: Mr R.S. Smith (coach), Mr W.J. Knight JP, R. Lamb, J. Phillips, L. Wheeler, F. Baxter, B. Samuel, E. Barber, Mr H. Holden, Mr G. Poulton. Middle row: B. Chambers, B. Williams, R. Vanassche, E. Barber (captain), I. Sealey (vice-captain), L. Holmberg, P. Walters. Front row: E. Rowe, E. Ingram.

The hunt at Godshill with the local constable, Phil Thatcher, following the hounds on his bicycle, 1960s. Constable Thatcher was one of the country's longest serving officers in any one village. He spent the whole of his service in Godshill with the exception of a small break for war service. Constable Thatcher retired in 1970.

Ventnor Cricket Club, 1919. Back row, left to right: E. Hess, (umpire), T. Pethick, W. Salaman, C. Cooper, W. Shannon, E.D. Carolis, H. Morris. Middle row: A.S. Hayward, W.G. Mitchell (captain), E. Watney (president), F.C.Y. Smith (secretary), W.J. Knight (asst. secretary). Front row: C.K. Lloyd, B. Goode.

Ventnor Cricket Club, 1926. Back row, left to right: A. Moorman, Nelson Love, George Brading, H. Bert, Len Lacey, Howard Brading, J.C. Rogers, Chas Nigh. Front row: Albert Buckett, Charlie Foxworthy, Vic Howell, Mr Sealey (president), Toby Hills, Ralph Eldridge, Ralph E. Savek.

Ventnor versus Shanklin cricket match, 27 June 1931. Back row, left to right: H. Williams, W. Lowe, E.D. Bowie, W.J. Knight, B. Bone, E.V. Howell, J.B. White, A. Dyer, S. Locke, N.V. Lowe, F. Craddock, A. Cook, F. Griffiths, R. Warder. Middle row: A.R. Gibbon, L. Williams, Capt. A. Cook (captain, Shanklin team), J.V. Hobbs, W.G. Mitchell (president), Mrs J.V. Hobbs, Dr L.G. Blair (captain, Ventnor team), Revd A.A.P. Winser, H.C. Brading, S. Penfold. Front row: L. Marshall, E. Rice.

Ventnor Cricket Club 1st XI, date unknown. Back row, left to right: R. Read (umpire), W. Bowe, W. Pound, E. Elgar, C.H. Denness (umpire). Middle row: W. Jeffery, G.H.S. Saunders, Dr V.J. Blake (captain), J. Morgan Richards Esq. (president), H. Greenhalgh (vice-captain), W.G. Mitchell, F.C.V. Smith (hon. secretary). Front row: D. Day, A.E. Batt.

Ventnor Cricket Club, triumphant in the J.H. League, 1908. Back row, left to right: F. Dyer, J.M. de Vine, Mr Gordon, S. Moorman, Mr Adcock, H. Jeffery, G. Torey. Middle row: F.C.Y. Smith, Revd G.F. Langford, W. Mew Judd, H. Greenhalgh, Dr Blake. Front row: H. Lincoln, W.G. Mitchell.

Ventnor Cricket Club, 1930. Back row, left to right: W. Lowe (umpire), L. Hess (hon. secretary), A.V. Howell, F. Burnett, H. Williams (scorer), W. Walker, N.V. Lowe. Front row: S. Locke, B. Bone, W.G. Mitchell (president), Dr L.G. Blair (captain), A. Dyer, W.J. Knight, H.C. Brading.

Ventnor Cricket Club, 1946. Back row, left to right: Jack Desmond, Charlie Sivier, B. White, Dyer jnr, Bob Dubber, Bill Peddar, 'Julie' Rogers, Bill Burden, Stan Locke, Pat Calvert, Roy Wearing, 'Vin' Marsh, Jack Bridges, Len Alvers, Sid Moorman, Tiller jnr, Freddie Waltham. Front row: Maj. Hawkins, Bill Steele, Ivor Bibby, Peter Mabey, John Owen, R. Wearing, Toby Dyer, Tommy Mackett, Ernie Turner, Ray Tiller, Freddy Watson, Charlie Rashley.

The Island Schoolboys football team, 1949. Back row, left to right: Jacobs, Hall, Gallop, Canham, Furmidge, Groundsell, Watts, O'Dell. Front row: Lines, Willis, Salter.

The opening of Ventnor Cricket Club's new pavilion. Unfortunately the date is not known.

BLACKGANG
& THE CHINE

I make no apologies for the fact that the final section of this book is devoted to the area of Blackgang and the Chine. Of all the parts of our garden isle which have seen great changes during the past two hundred years, Blackgang and the Chine has suffered the most.

The very word 'Blackgang' has a sinister ring to it, probably conjuring up images of wreckers and smugglers working down on the storm-lashed shores. It certainly had more than its share of all of these. Smuggling was practised on a large scale, shipwrecks

Alexander Dabell, founder of Britain's first theme park in 1842.

Blackgang Chine, showing the chine and cliffs on either side of the gorge, c. 1901.

were many and legends abounded. One in particular was that of a hermit monk from St Catherine's Oratory; in the Middle Ages he fought a battle of words with the evil Giant of Chale, who for many years had defiled the area. Good triumphed over evil and the giant was no more, but the monk cursed the ground on which the giant had walked. Part of the curse was as follows: 'And the earth it shall crumble and crumble away. And crumble on till judgement day.' Legend or not, it does just that, at the rate of about 8 ft a year. Has the curse anything to do with the erosion? Have the words of the holy man justified the cause in the minds of the superstitious? In recent times a much more feasible explanation has been given by geologists, who have confirmed that the area is built on blue slipper, or blue clay. After heavy rain it dries out and crumbles, taking yards of cliff with it, buildings and all.

In the early 1800s Blackgang Chine was a steep ravine stretching over half a mile down to the shore, a wild and desolate place only visited by mackerel fishermen such as the Wheelers of Chale Bay during the mackerel season.

In 1923 Alexander Dabell and his family moved to the island from Nottingham and by 1830 had a successful business in Newport, but Alexander was very much an entrepreneur and soon started up hair-dressing and gift shops all over the island. To advertise his businesses he walked around the towns and villages with a chained bear.

In 1842 he negotiated the lease of the land at Blackgang. He landscaped the area and built a small kiosk which sold tea and sticky buns to the Victorian gentlemen and their ladies out for their Sunday afternoon stroll. Soon afterwards he purchased a huge whale

By the 1920s Blackgang Chine had become a popular tourist attraction. Here visitors are arriving by coach from Ventnor, 4 September 1922.

which had died after being washed up at The Needles. He sold the blubber and had the bones bleached and displayed in a hut which he built at the Chine for all to see. At the same time his wife Amelia opened a gift bazaar – the Blackgang Chine Theme Park had begun. It is said that it became Britain's first true theme park, and since 1933, when the first funny mirrors were installed, the company has invested in many award-winning features and exhibitions.

Today the fourth and fifth generations of the Dabell family continue to fight the landslides. Fortunately they own a great deal of acreage inland from the cliff edge and each year they can 'build back' and are able to site various attractions on this area. They also carefully monitor the movement of the earth there. Unfortunately those who live in the village of Blackgang and the surrounding area, and whose houses and bungalows were once many hundreds of yards inland, now have to take their chances with nature. Back doors, gardens and patios are now perched on the cliff edge and are poised to slide, albeit sometimes gracefully, down to the storm-washed beaches. Many times this has happened within minutes or overnight.

Walter Dabell, son of Alexander, 1890. When Alexander died in 1898 he left the business to his wife. One year later Walter married and entered the business, eventually living 'over the shop' in the Chine Bungalow. Frances and Walter had a son, Bruce, who joined the staff in 1920. It was he who was mainly responsible for the planning of the many tableaux we are able to enjoy today.

Unfortunately we are unable to ascertain the name of the coach driver who, it seems, has been invited to tea with friends in the gnome garden, *c.* 1950.

A typical mackerel-fishing scene in Chale Bay, 1910. The mackerel season is quite short and the fishermen have to endure rough, chilly weather. The huts on the beach are where they used to stay.

The Great Dinosaur Lift, 1971. The directors of the theme park, realizing the potential of the growing interest in dinosaurs and fossil hunting, especially on the Isle of Wight, created a dinosaur park. The models were scaled down in size but still had to be lifted into their positions by helicopter, hence the event's name.

Isolene and Josephine Dabell with one of their staff at the entrance to Blackgang Chine, 1950. The admission price was then 6*d* and remained so for many years. Note the request to put the money in the box should no attendant be available. Blackgang Theme Park has always maintained that the entrance fee is all that has to be paid – except, of course, if you are an addict of the 'penny' machines in the arcade.

BLACKGANG CHINE

THE FRAGRANT MINUTE.

Some ramblers start at Ventnor, and walk it, all the way.
Others go from Shanklin (I did the other day).
And if I must be truthful, I went by motor car,
But for stalwart, honest hikers, the distance isn't far !

And oh ! when you get there, you'll gasp out your delight,
This Chine is quite unusual, a most impressive sight.
Blue clay and yellow sandstone towering above the sea,
Silent, grim and scornful—gigantic masonry.

Take the ascending pathway to the Observation Peak.
On the wooden platform stand—but do not speak.
'Tis the best feature of this Blackgang Chine.
In this lovely Island, no view half so fine
As seen from this pinnacle when the day is clear.
Boldly stand the Needles—and Dorset's coast draws near.

(Reprinted by permission of Wilhelmina Stitch, author of " The Fragrant Minute." " Silken Threads." " Silver Linings." and many other booklets.)

A tribute to Blackgang by island poet Wilhelmina Stitch. The poem is a great favourite with residents and visitors alike.

In addition to mackerel fishing, Blackgang and Chale Bay were originally famous for smuggling and wrecking. This photograph was taken in 1897, when fencing and pathways show it was already established as a tourist attraction. Now the smugglers and wreckers have given way to dinosaurs and Red Indians.

The Blackgang Hotel, 1930. The friendship of the landlord and Alexander Dabell way back in 1839 sparked off the idea of creating the tea gardens. The site is now a large cafeteria and living quarters.

Lowcliff and Cliff Terrace, Chale, showing the golf links, 1909.

The Blackgang Chine gorge in 1920, when visitors to the park could make their way down to the beach by way of the wooden stairway and rustic bridge. This area has long since been eroded and the beach is no longer accessible.

Blackgang Chine gift shop, at the entrance to the Chine, was set up inside the skeleton of a fin whale. The whale had died when it was beached at The Needles in 1843. Alexander Dabell bought it at auction, sold the blubber, bleached the bones and it rapidly took its place at the Chine entrance.

The skeleton of yet another whale beached near Blackgang in 1924. Whales and dolphins are frequent visitors to the island and sometimes become stranded. Luckily today's technology allows us to help them quickly back into the water.

The Lower Blackgang Chine tea rooms, 1890s. Built for Alexander Dabell in 1845, the tea rooms sat halfway down the cliff. It was a long climb down for Victorian, and later Edwardian, residents and visitors, but they seemed to enjoy it.

Blackgang and a continuation of the pathway leading past the tea rooms and down to the beach, 1891.

Fishermen's Cottage at Blackgang Chine, 1923. Long since washed into the sea, this cottage was used by fishermen during the mackerel season.

A view of the Undercliff from Windy Corner, 1900. Windy Corner, as the name implies, was one part of Blackgang which would take the full force of the hurricane- and gale-force winds, so prevalent on the island.

The golf links at Blackgang, 1913. This is believed to be one of the last pictures taken of the links before they were given over to the first Isle of Wight Home Guard in 1914.

Southlands, 1909. This great house was demolished in 1910 to prevent it from falling on to the beach. People say that they saw falcons and jackdaws vacate their perches on Windy Corner as if with one accord. Hours later 120,000 tons of rock cracked, moaned and slipped down into a watery grave.

Windy Corner at the Undercliff, *c.* 1900.

A photograph taken just after the Rockend landslide, 23 July 1928. The newly formed undercliff, composed of a muddy sea of rocks and uprooted trees, took months to settle, and then the land moved again.

This monument situated behind Blackgang, has already been briefly mentioned on page 55. It is known locally as 'The Russian Monument' and was erected by Michael Hoy to commemorate the visit to Britain in 1814 of Tsar Alexander I of Russia. A businessman and entrepreneur, Hoy had made a fortune in St Petersburg before turning his talents to London and the Isle of Wight, where he owned many properties. He died in 1828. Subsequently, W.H. Dawes put a plaque on the north face of the pillar's base in memory of British troops who fell in the Crimean War. Maybe Dawes was annoyed at the tribute paid to the tsar!

The Wheeler family enjoying a summer on the beach, making and repairing their nets and tackle in readiness for the coming season, 1900.

The Wheeler family in Wheelers Bay, 1879. The bay was so named because the Wheelers had fished there for hundreds of years. Although quite a respected family, this photograph shows the spartan conditions in which they lived.

ACKNOWLEDGEMENTS

This book would not have been possible but for the assistance given by many people. Therefore, I would like to thank the following: R. Abbott; Brian and Marian Bates, the Landlord and Landlady of Raffles Tavern, Bembridge; Gwen Best; Simon Dabell, Director of Blackgang Chine Theme Park; Fr Davey, Priest in Charge of Our Lady and St Wilfred's Church, Ventnor; Bert Draper; Dr A. Insole; Malcolm Johnson; A.R. Lacey; Audrey Moore; A. Morey; M.A. Nicholson; D. Nobbs; Bill Patten; T. Roberts; Revd F.A. Royle, Minister of Chale Methodist Church; J. Saunders of St Boniface County Primary School; E. Thatcher of Ventnor Cricket Club; Ventnor Heritage; Cllr J. Walters of Wroxall; J. Whittington; Mrs Williams, Headmistress of Godshill County Primary School; Wroxall County Primary School.

Finally, for all his help in the preparation of the book I would like to thank my friend and colleague, Peter T.G. White.

...wyth & North Ceredigion
...Abingdon

...ey: A Second Selection
...he Avon from Stratford to
...esbury
...ham
...nam
...Amesbury
...ey
...& Bestwood
...& Bestwood: A Second
...tion
...l & the Arun Valley
...rne
...Ashby-de-la-Zouch
...ircraft
...ury
...& Tooting
...yshire
...Mortlake & Sheen
...ey

...sfield
...d
...dshire at Work
...rth
...ey

...rd

...gham Railways
...'s Stortford &
...ridgeworth
...stone & Seaford
...stone & Seaford: A Second
...tion
...Country Aviation
...Country Railways
...Country Road Transport
...urn
...ool
...d Blandford Forum
...ley

...emouth
...rd
...ree & Bocking at Work
...a
...wood
...water & the River Parrett
...gton
...rt & the Bride Valley
...ey Hill
...on & Hove
...on & Hove: A Second
...tion
...l
...d Bristol
...n & Norwood
...Broadstairs & St Peters
...ey, Keston & Hayes

Buckingham & District
Burford
Bury
Bushbury
Camberwell
Cambridge
Cannock Yesterday & Today
Canterbury: A Second Selection
Castle Combe to Malmesbury
Chadwell Heath
Chard & Ilminster
Chatham Dockyard
Chatham & Gillingham
Cheadle
Cheam & Belmont
Chelmsford
Cheltenham: A Second Selection
Cheltenham at War
Cheltenham in the 1950s
Chepstow & the River Wye
Chesham Yesterday & Today
Cheshire Railways
Chester
Chippenham & Lacock
Chiswick
Chorley & District
Cirencester
Around Cirencester
Clacton-on-Sea
Around Clitheroe
Clwyd Railways
Clydesdale
Colchester
Colchester 1940–70
Colyton & Seaton
The Cornish Coast
Corsham & Box
The North Cotswolds
Coventry: A Second Selection
Around Coventry
Cowes & East Cowes
Crawley New Town
Around Crawley
Crewkerne & the Ham Stone
  Villages
Cromer
Croydon
Crystal Palace, Penge & Anerley
Darlington
Darlington: A Second Selection
Dawlish & Teignmouth
Deal
Derby
Around Devizes
Devon Aerodromes
East Devon at War
Around Didcot & the Hagbournes
Dorchester
Douglas
Dumfries
Dundee at Work
Durham People

Durham at Work
Ealing & Northfields
East Grinstead
East Ham
Eastbourne
Elgin
Eltham
Ely
Enfield
Around Epsom
Esher
Evesham to Bredon
Exeter
Exmouth & Budleigh Salterton
Fairey Aircraft
Falmouth
Farnborough
Farnham: A Second Selection
Fleetwood
Folkestone: A Second Selection
Folkestone: A Third Selection
The Forest of Dean
Frome
Fulham
Galashiels
Garsington
Around Garstang
Around Gillingham
Gloucester
Gloucester: from the Walwin
  Collection
North Gloucestershire at War
South Gloucestershire at War
Gosport
Goudhurst to Tenterden
Grantham
Gravesend
Around Gravesham
Around Grays
Great Yarmouth
Great Yarmouth: A Second
  Selection
Greenwich & Woolwich
Grimsby
Around Grimsby
Grimsby Docks
Gwynedd Railways
Hackney: A Second Selection
Hackney: A Third Selection
From Haldon to Mid-Dartmoor
Hammersmith & Shepherds Bush
Hampstead to Primrose Hill
Harrow & Pinner
Hastings
Hastings: A Second Selection
Haverfordwest
Hayes & West Drayton
Around Haywards Heath
Around Heathfield
Around Heathfield: A Second
  Selection
Around Helston

Around Henley-on-Thames
Herefordshire
Herne Bay
Heywood
The High Weald
The High Weald: A Second
  Selection
Around Highworth
Around Highworth & Faringdon
Hitchin
Holderness
Honiton & the Otter Valley
Horsham & District
Houghton-le-Spring &
  Hetton-le-Hole
Houghton-le-Spring & Hetton-le-
  Hole: A Second Selection
Huddersfield: A Second Selection
Huddersfield: A Third Selection
Ilford
Ilfracombe
Ipswich: A Second Selection
Islington
Jersey: A Third Selection
Kendal
Kensington & Chelsea
East Kent at War
Keswick & the Central Lakes
Around Keynsham & Saltford
The Changing Face of Keynsham
Kingsbridge
Kingston
Kinver
Kirkby & District
Kirkby Lonsdale
Around Kirkham
Knowle & Dorridge
The Lake Counties at Work
Lancashire
The Lancashire Coast
Lancashire North of the Sands
Lancashire Railways
East Lancashire at War
Around Lancaster
Lancing & Sompting
Around Leamington Spa
Around Leamington Spa:
  A Second Selection
Leeds in the News
Leeds Road & Rail
Around Leek
Leicester
The Changing Face of Leicester
Leicester at Work
Leicestershire People
Around Leighton Buzzard &
  Linslade
Letchworth
Lewes
Lewisham & Deptford:
  A Second Selection
Lichfield

Lincoln
Lincoln Cathedral
The Lincolnshire Coast
Liverpool
Around Llandudno
Around Lochaber
Theatrical London
Around Louth
The Lower Fal Estuary
Lowestoft
Luton
Lympne Airfield
Lytham St Annes
Maidenhead
Around Maidenhead
Around Malvern
Manchester
Manchester Road & Rail
Mansfield
Marlborough: A Second Selection
Marylebone & Paddington
Around Matlock
Melton Mowbray
Around Melksham
The Mendips
Merton & Morden
Middlesbrough
Midsomer Norton & Radstock
Around Mildenhall
Milton Keynes
Minehead
Monmouth & the River Wye
The Nadder Valley
Newark
Around Newark
Newbury
Newport, Isle of Wight
The Norfolk Broads
Norfolk at War
North Fylde
North Lambeth
North Walsham & District
Northallerton
Northampton
Around Norwich
Nottingham 1944–74
The Changing Face of Nottingham
Victorian Nottingham
Nottingham Yesterday & Today
Nuneaton
Around Oakham
Ormskirk & District
Otley & District
Oxford: The University
Oxford Yesterday & Today
Oxfordshire Railways: A Second
    Selection
Oxfordshire at School
Around Padstow
Pattingham & Wombourne

Penwith
Penzance & Newlyn
Around Pershore
Around Plymouth
Poole
Portsmouth
Poulton-le-Fylde
Preston
Prestwich
Pudsey
Radcliffe
RAF Chivenor
RAF Cosford
RAF Hawkinge
RAF Manston
RAF Manston: A Second Selection
RAF St Mawgan
RAF Tangmere
Ramsgate & Thanet Life
Reading
Reading: A Second Selection
Redditch & the Needle District
Redditch: A Second Selection
Richmond, Surrey
Rickmansworth
Around Ripley
The River Soar
Romney Marsh
Romney Marsh: A Second
    Selection
Rossendale
Around Rotherham
Rugby
Around Rugeley
Ruislip
Around Ryde
St Albans
St Andrews
Salford
Salisbury
Salisbury: A Second Selection
Salisbury: A Third Selection
Around Salisbury
Sandhurst & Crowthorne
Sandown & Shanklin
Sandwich
Scarborough
Scunthorpe
Seaton, Lyme Regis & Axminster
Around Seaton & Sidmouth
Sedgley & District
The Severn Vale
Sherwood Forest
Shrewsbury
Shrewsbury: A Second Selection
Shropshire Railways
Skegness
Around Skegness
Skipton & the Dales
Around Slough

Smethwick
Somerton & Langport
Southampton
Southend-on-Sea
Southport
Southwark
Southwell
Southwold to Aldeburgh
Stafford
Around Stafford
Staffordshire Railways
Around Staveley
Stepney
Stevenage
The History of Stilton Cheese
Stoke-on-Trent
Stoke Newington
Stonehouse to Painswick
Around Stony Stratford
Around Stony Stratford: A Second
    Selection
Stowmarket
Streatham
Stroud & the Five Valleys
Stroud & the Five Valleys: A
    Second Selection
Stroud's Golden Valley
The Stroudwater and Thames &
    Severn Canals
The Stroudwater and Thames &
    Severn Canals: A Second
    Selection
Suffolk at Work
Suffolk at Work: A Second
    Selection
The Heart of Suffolk
Sunderland
Sutton
Swansea
Swindon: A Third Selection
Swindon: A Fifth Selection
Around Tamworth
Taunton
Around Taunton
Teesdale
Teesdale: A Second Selection
Tenbury Wells
Around Tettenhall & Codshall
Tewkesbury & the Vale of
    Gloucester
Thame to Watlington
Around Thatcham
Around Thirsk
Thornbury to Berkeley
Tipton
Around Tonbridge
Trowbridge
Around Truro
TT Races
Tunbridge Wells

Tunbridge Wells: A Second
    Selection
Twickenham
Uley, Dursley & Cam
The Upper Fal
The Upper Tywi Valley
Uxbridge, Hillingdon & Cow
The Vale of Belvoir
The Vale of Conway
Ventnor
Wakefield
Wallingford
Walsall
Waltham Abbey
Wandsworth at War
Wantage, Faringdon & the V
    Villages
Around Warwick
Weardale
Weardale: A Second Selectio
Wednesbury
Wells
Welshpool
West Bromwich
West Wight
Weston-super-Mare
Around Weston-super-Mare
Weymouth & Portland
Around Wheatley
Around Whetstone
Whitchurch to Market Dray
Around Whitstable
Wigton & the Solway Plain
Willesden
Around Wilton
Wimbledon
Around Windsor
Wingham, Addisham &
    Littlebourne
Wisbech
Witham & District
Witney
Around Witney
The Witney District
Wokingham
Around Woodbridge
Around Woodstock
Woolwich
Woolwich Royal Arsenal
Around Wootton Bassett,
    Cricklade & Purton
Worcester
Worcester in a Day
Around Worcester
Worcestershire at Work
Around Worthing
Wotton-under-Edge to Chipp
    Sodbury
Wymondham & Attleborough
The Yorkshire Wolds

To order any of these titles please telephone our distributor, Littlehampton Book Services on 01903 7215
For a catalogue of these and our other titles please ring Regina Schinner on 01453 731114